**Grow Your Confidence**

GROW YOUR CONFIDENCE

An Hachette UK Company
www.hachette.co.uk

Vie Books, an imprint of Summersdale Publishers Ltd
Part of Octopus Publishing Group Limited
Carmelite House
50 Victoria Embankment
LONDON
EC4Y 0DZ
UK

www.summersdale.com

Printed and bound in Poland

ISBN: 978-1-83799-171-6

Substantial discounts on bulk quantities of Summersdale books are available to corporations, professional associations and other organizations. For details contact general enquiries: telephone: +44 (0) 1243 771107 or email: enquiries@summersdale.com.

Neither the author nor the publisher can be held responsible for any injury, loss or claim – be it health, financial or otherwise – arising out of the use, or misuse, of the suggestions made herein. None of the opinions or suggestions in this book are intended to replace medical opinion. If you have concerns about your health or that of a child in your care, please seek professional advice.

# Grow Your Confidence

## A Child's Guide to Finding Courage

### POPPY O'NEILL

# Contents

# Foreword

*By Amanda Ashman-Wymbs, Counsellor and Psychotherapist,
registered and accredited by the British Association for
Counselling and Psychotherapy*

Having raised two daughters and working therapeutically with young people for over 15 years, it is clear that confidence issues are affecting our children and their lives in many ways, limiting their experiences and eroding their strong natural sense of self.

Knowing how to support a child to work through these issues can sometimes be confusing and overwhelming for parents and carers. Poppy O'Neill's *Grow Your Confidence* is an easy-to-read, supportive and enjoyable workbook to give children the tools they need to enable their self-confidence journeys. Children can use this independently or with the support of their parent or carer.

Full of fun activities and insightful information to help raise a child's awareness and understanding of their emotions, this book offers a step-by-step guide towards overcoming low confidence by offering techniques, such as affirmations, emotional literacy and having a growth mindset, for the child to use. It normalizes their experiences and helps them learn to practise mindfulness. It also shows children the connection of feeling good from self-care in the form of sleep, diet, exercise and time spent in nature. *Grow Your Confidence* encourages self-compassion, empathy for others and conversational engagement with their trusted grown-up, all of which bring a greater feeling of connection that help children grow confidence naturally.

In my opinion this is a much-needed book that will greatly help support many children to grow their confidence in today's challenging world.

# Introduction:
# A guide for parents and carers

Inspired and informed by therapeutic methods used by child psychologists, this book is your child's guide to believing in themselves and feeling confident. Inside you'll find easy-to-understand ideas and information about how our minds and emotions work, as well as simple, fun activities that will help your child engage with the topic.

If your child seems to hang back, is always a little unsure of themselves and gets easily put off from trying new things, they may be in need of support in growing their confidence. As much as you love and encourage them, some children can really struggle with self-doubt. That's the difficult thing about confidence: it's not about feeling no self-doubt – it's about keeping calm and acting with courage even when deep down we feel scared, silly or shy.

Aimed at children aged 7–11, this book will help give your child a new perspective on confidence and learn that they can be themselves and be confident at the same time. It's also full of tips and tricks for boosting confidence when you need it most.

If your child struggles with self-doubt and low confidence, rest assured that you're not alone. Over the next few pages you'll find more information on how to support your child to get the most out of this book, and at the back of the book there's a conclusion for parents and carers that's packed with advice.

# Signs of low confidence

Even the most confident people experience self-doubt sometimes, and it's normal for confidence levels to go up and down depending on where we are, who we're with and all sorts of other factors. However, a lack of confidence can be very distressing, especially for children. Here are some signs to look out for that your child could be having a hard time with their self-confidence:

- They are reluctant or struggle to make friends
- They are very critical of themselves and others
- They find it very difficult to cope with small mistakes
- They are very sensitive to what others think of them
- They find it difficult to express their feelings
- It is very important to them to fit in and be like their peers
- The idea of failure is very stressful to them

If this sounds like your child, don't panic. Confidence isn't something that comes naturally to everyone, and there are lots of ways you can gently support your child to build their self-belief.

# How to talk to your child about confidence

Talking and listening to your child is one of the most powerful ways you can support their self-confidence. When children express their feelings and we meet them with acceptance and understanding, their confidence grows.

At its heart, confidence is about taking a risk and feeling relaxed about how it will turn out. When we know we will be OK even if we fail, it gets a lot easier to act with confidence. All sorts of things can feel risky – we risk our feelings every time we try to make a new friend, share something we've created or admit to something we feel embarrassed about.

When your child comes to you with something they're struggling with, show them understanding. If you can, share a moment from your life when you felt similarly. For a child having a hard time, it can seem like everybody else has effortless confidence – showing them that they're not alone is a great place to start the conversation.

## Using this book with your child

This book is for your child, so let them take the lead. They might like lots of guidance and to look at the activities together, or they might prefer to work through it more independently. Letting them be in charge and reassuring them that there are no wrong answers will contribute to developing their confidence.

When your child feels good about themselves they are better equipped to deal with the challenges of everyday life. Let them know that you believe in them and that you're there for them if they need you.

I hope this book helps grow your child's confidence and boost their sense of self-belief. However, if you have any serious concerns about your child's mental health, your doctor is the best person to go to for further advice.

# Welcome to Grow Your Confidence

Welcome to *Grow Your Confidence*, a guide to shrinking self-doubt and learning the key to unlock your confidence. If you're reading this book, you probably feel shy sometimes or find it hard to believe in yourself. Even if, on the outside, everybody else seems super-confident, the truth is we all feel self-doubt sometimes.

This book is packed with information and activities to help you learn all about confidence and how it works. It's not a mystical thing you're either born with or not – the key to growing your confidence is already inside you. Plus, there are handy tips and tricks for boosting your confidence when you need it most.

# How to use this book: A guide for children

This book is for you if you often…

⭐ Find it hard to speak up

⭐ Feel scared to try new things

⭐ Feel very uncomfortable when the attention is on you

⭐ Worry that things will go wrong

⭐ Feel like you're the only one who finds things difficult

Perhaps this sounds like you most of the time, or just some of the time. Either way, this book is here to help you grow your confidence so you can face challenges with courage. Inside you'll find lots of interesting ideas and information about confidence, plus fun activities to help you learn about how it all works.

If there's any part of this book you're not sure about, or want to talk over with someone, you can ask a trusted grown-up to look at it with you.

This book is about you and your self-confidence, so there are no wrong answers and *you* are the expert!

## Meet the *Grow Your Confidence* gang!

Throughout this book you'll find kids from the *Grow Your Confidence* gang popping up to guide you through the activities, learning how to face challenges bravely and grow their confidence alongside you.

# Part 1:
# Confidence explained

Sometimes it seems like everybody in the world has loads and loads of confidence – but what exactly is it? Where does it come from and can anyone grow their confidence? In this chapter we'll discover the answers.

# I am as unique as my fingerprint

We all have fingerprints and each fingerprint is one of a kind. This is just one of the many ways that humans are connected and different at the same time. No one else has a fingerprint quite like yours – even if you are an identical twin! Just like our fingerprints, no one is quite like you, and that's a very special thing. Understanding that we are unique and also have lots in common with those around us is the first step to growing confidence.

Can you colour in all the white space on this fingerprint?

**Try looking at your fingerprint through a magnifying glass – can you see all the swirls and shapes?**

# What is confidence?

When we feel confident, we feel sure that what we're doing will turn out OK. Someone might feel confident in their…

- Singing voice
- Maths knowledge
- Bike riding
- Football skills

… or any number of things – usually things they've practised and built skills in over a long period of time. This kind of confidence comes from practice and experience of doing well already. If we've already done something well, our brains understand that we'll probably do it well again.

So how do people feel confident trying something new for the first time? The answer is: they don't feel confident – they act confident.

In order to collect experiences that will help us feel confident in the future, we need to try things we don't feel confident about yet.

Acting with confidence simply means staying as calm as you can while doing something brave.

Let's try an experiment – we're going to take a measurement of your confidence levels. All you need is a coloured pen or pencil. Are you ready?

Read the situations and colour in the bar to show how confident you feel that this would go OK. For example, Ben isn't feeling very confident about asking for help, so his confidence bar looks like this:

Ask for help
with a problem

Stand up for myself
against a bully

Join a new club where
I don't know anybody

Perform a speaking
role in a school play

Go into a shop and
buy something

Perhaps your confidence levels are about the same for all of those situations, or perhaps they're quite different. All of these things take bravery, so it makes sense to find any or all of them hard.

I can
do things
that seem
hard

# I feel confident when...

Can you think of a time you feel very confident? It might be when you are playing a game or using a skill you've practised a lot, or maybe there's a person you love spending time with who makes you feel confident in yourself.

Write or draw about when you feel confident here:

# What are emotions?

"Emotion" is another word for a feeling. The four main emotions are:

- ☆ Happiness
- ☆ Sadness
- ☆ Fear
- ☆ Anger

But there are lots more! We feel emotions in our bodies, and they can feel small and quiet or big and loud. Some feelings feel nice and some feel uncomfortable. Everyone has feelings, even if they don't always show them.

It's OK to feel whatever you are feeling, even if it's uncomfortable – like sadness or anger. Feelings are changeable and they don't have to stick around for ages. You can imagine them passing through your body as a cloud passes through the sky.

What does confidence feel like? When we feel truly confident, we feel peaceful, calm and sure.

What does bravery feel like? When we're growing our confidence, we often have to act with bravery. Bravery feels like strength, power and determination.

# Activity: How my heart feels

This heart is divided into six sections. Use coloured pens or pencils to make each section match the feeling. Everyone experiences emotions a bit differently, so it's OK to pick whichever colour, pattern or picture feels right to you for each section.

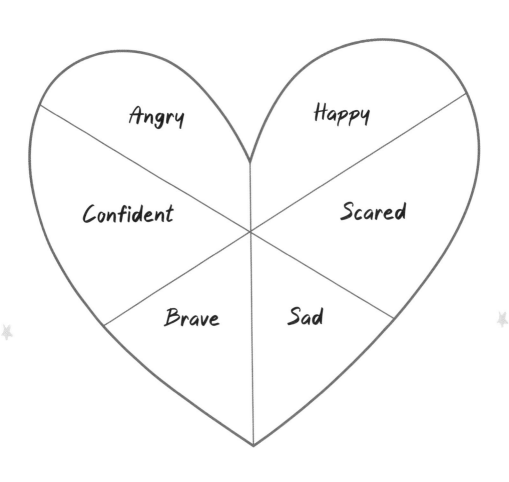

# Part 1: Confidence explained

Now that you've coloured in the heart, take a moment to think about how you feel right now. It might be one emotion, or a mix. You might not have quite the right words for how you feel right now, and that's OK too.

You could describe how your body feels, or draw any images that reflect your emotions.

Write or draw how you feel right now here:

# What is self-doubt?

Self-doubt is the opposite of confidence. Self-doubt makes you feel very unsure that you'll be OK at something.

When we feel self-doubt, our brains imagine that we'll fail or mess up. It shrinks our confidence and makes it a lot harder to find bravery and act boldly.

We can feel self-doubt even about a skill that we've practised a lot. Here's a story to help explain why.

*Enzo and Sam are playing a game of basketball this afternoon. Enzo has been playing basketball for two years and is very skilled at it. Sam has never tried basketball – today will be her first time.*

*Enzo has encouraged Sam to play basketball with him because they're best friends and he wants to share his favourite sport with her. Sam doesn't feel very confident because she hasn't had any practice, but she knows it'll be fun because Enzo will be there. She knows it's OK that she doesn't have basketball skills yet.*

*Just before the game, a child who is often to mean to other kids came up to him. He said all sorts of mean things to Enzo about his basketball skills and about how Enzo looks. The child really hurt Enzo's feelings.*

*Now, Enzo's confidence is very low and he doesn't believe he'll have fun and score any points in the game.*

*The bully's words have shrunk Enzo's confidence and grown his self-doubt. Seeing Enzo get treated unkindly makes Sam's confidence shrink too.*

**Make sure you tell a trusted grown-up if someone is being mean to you.**

Did you notice how unkind words
from someone else shrunk Enzo's confidence,
even though he had lots of practice and
experience to help him feel confident?

# What can shrink your confidence?

It might feel like there are lots of things that can shrink your confidence and grow your self-doubt. For Enzo, it was the bully's words that made him feel small and doubt his basketball skills. Trying to shrink someone else's confidence is a very unkind thing to do.

Here are some other things that can shrink our confidence:

- A bad experience in the past
- Thinking something terrible will happen if you don't do well
- Feeling sad, scared or angry about something
- Worrying that you'll be laughed at
- Not getting enough sleep
- Not eating nutritious food
- Not having enough to drink
- Seeing other people get treated unkindly

Keep reading to find lots of clever ways to shrink self-doubt down to size.

When we need to act with confidence, it can help to imagine our most confident self. Think about how confident you felt on page 20 and imagine you could call upon those confidence powers any time you wanted... like a superhero!

What would your confidence powers allow you to do? Write or draw your amazing powers here:

Can you add patterns and colour to this superhero costume?

When you need a boost of confidence, imagine yourself as your super-confident, superhero self!

# I am a superhero!

# Part 2: How to grow your confidence

Confidence grows slowly and steadily – there's no rush. It's OK if you don't feel very confident about certain things, or a lot of things! Everybody has their own unique strengths and challenges. In this chapter you'll learn how to find your inner confidence and help it grow, one step at a time.

# Let your mind grow

Growing your confidence starts with believing in yourself. This might sound like quite a big idea, but all it takes is some small changes to how you think about yourself and the challenges you face. If we only think self-doubting thoughts, it's very difficult to find the bravery to prove those thoughts wrong.

The small changes we can make to let our confident thoughts grow are sometimes called a "growth mindset". This idea was invented by Carol Dweck and it's really interesting!

Having a growth mindset means we believe we can always learn, grow and change. When we have a growth mindset, challenges and mistakes don't feel so scary because we know we can bounce back and try again.

## Growth mindset

*I can try again*

*I improve with practice*

*Mistakes help me learn*

*I can ask for help*

The opposite of a growth mindset is a fixed mindset: where we believe we need to be perfect, that we cannot change and that if something is hard we should avoid it.

## Fixed mindset

I should already
be perfect

I give up

I want to
avoid making
mistakes

I'll never
be good
enough

A growth mindset will help you grow your confidence by practising it! Keep reading to find out how…

# There is only one me

# My challenges

Are there certain things that you feel very low confidence about? Perhaps it's one of the ideas you measured on page 18 or different things entirely.

Joseph feels a lot of self-doubt about tests. His favourite subject is maths, and usually he feels confident and looks forward to maths lessons. But as soon as the teacher says there will be a test in maths class, his confidence levels drop.

Youssef feels OK about tests, but he really struggles with feeling confident about maths.

Julia is confident in her maths knowledge and feels OK about tests, but a bully has been unkind to her on the way to school.

Joseph, Youssef and Julia all feel low confidence about the maths test, for different reasons! They are all facing different challenges to their confidence levels.

# The circle of confidence

Imagine confidence is like a circle inside you. The things you feel confident about are inside the circle, and your challenges are outside of the circle.

Here's Emma's circle of confidence:

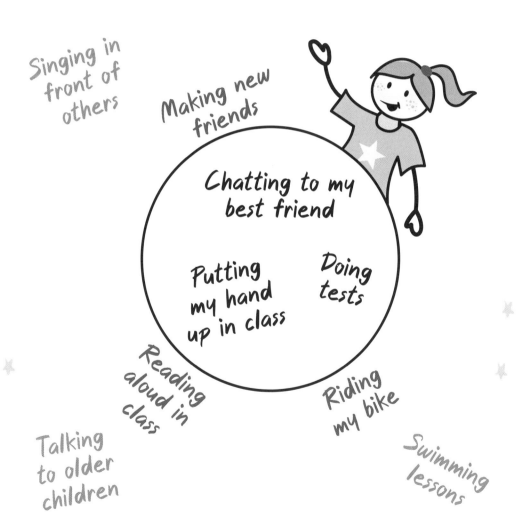

Can you see how some of the things are just outside the circle of confidence, while others are quite far away? The further away from the circle of confidence, the bigger the challenge and the more bravery is needed to give these things a go. Imagine this is your very own circle of confidence. Inside the circle, add your strengths and the things you feel confident about.

Outside the circle, add your challenges – the things that take bravery for you to do. Remember – the further away from the circle, the bigger the challenge.

You can add as many strengths and challenges as you like.

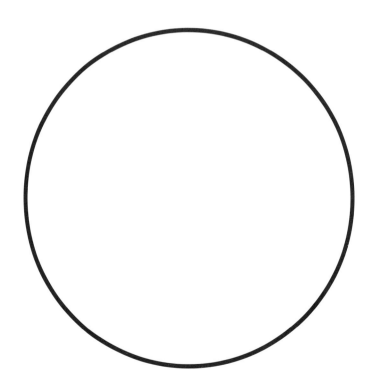

# I can take one step at a time

# Growing your circle of confidence

When something is a huge challenge and takes a lot of bravery, you don't have to leap straight from your circle of confidence all the way to your challenge.

The wonderful thing about our circle of confidence is how stretchy it is. When we stay inside the circle but stretch the edge of it, our circle grows bigger. The more our circle grows, the more things we feel comfortable and confident about.

Let's pick one of Emma's big challenges on page 35 – swimming lessons. Instead of leaping out of her circle of confidence all the way to her challenge, Emma has drawn a line. She adds ideas to the line, thinking about ways she could take steps towards swimming lessons while stretching her circle of confidence.

Each step Emma takes to stretch her circle of confidence takes bravery. She goes slowly, feeling her confidence grow with each new step.

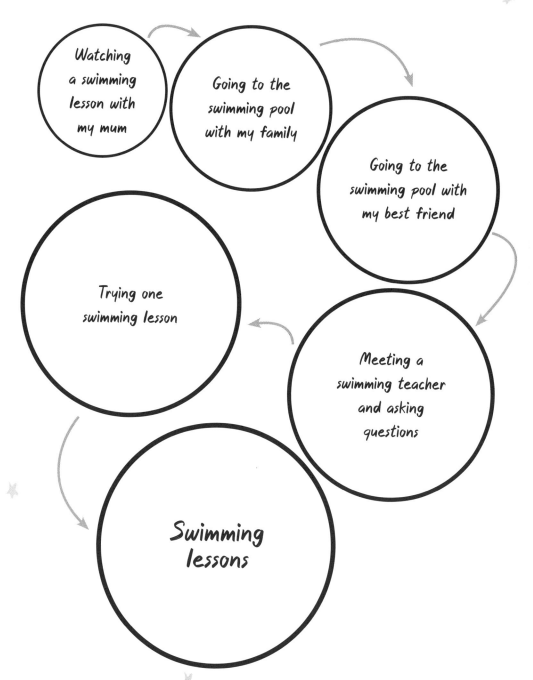

Watching a swimming lesson with my mum

Going to the swimming pool with my family

Going to the swimming pool with my best friend

Trying one swimming lesson

Meeting a swimming teacher and asking questions

Swimming lessons

**The reasons why something is a big challenge will be different for everybody, so if swimming lessons is one of your challenges, your brave steps might be different, and that's OK.**

Have a go at coming up with some brave steps to stretch your circle of confidence. Start by picking one challenge and write it in the circle. Then write down all the steps you can take to help you feel braver and make the challenge more achievable.

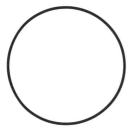

Remember, you are the expert on what is brave and challenging for you, so there are no wrong answers.

# Using mindfulness

Mindfulness means focusing your attention on what is happening right in this moment, and letting thoughts about the past or future go quiet for a while. It's a really helpful tool when taking brave steps towards your challenges.

Taking brave steps can feel difficult when we focus on the big challenge we're working towards. With mindfulness, we can forget the big challenge and think only about what is happening now. This helps us find our bravery.

Here are some mindful exercises you can use to help you focus on the now:

## My five senses

Check in with each of your senses, one by one:

✧ What can you see?

✧ What can you hear?

✧ What can you touch?

✧ What can you taste?

✧ What can you smell?

Our senses are our connection with the world. Use them to take in all the interesting details!

## Take deep, mindful breaths

1. Breathe in through your nose, filling your lungs with air.

2. Notice how the air feels as it travels through your nostrils and into your lungs.

3. Breathe out slowly through your nose.

4. Notice how the air feels warmer on its way out of your nostrils.

5. Keep going for three breaths.

## Mindful hands

Take a moment to look at the palms of your hands. You'll find there's plenty to see!

When we spend time noticing the small details that we don't often pay attention to, we are being mindful.

Can you add some of the details you find on your palm to this hand?

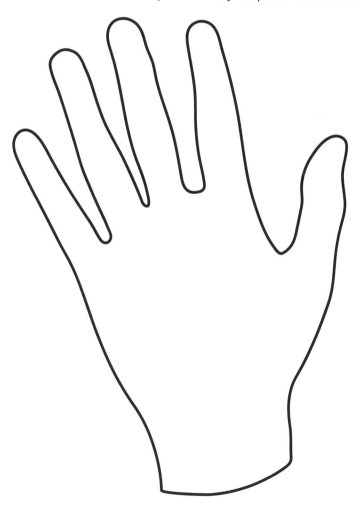

# Talking to a trusted grown-up

Whatever your strengths, challenges and confidence levels are, talking to a trusted grown-up will help you feel more confident. This is because when we feel like another person understands our struggles and bravery, our confidence grows.

Talking about how you are feeling and what's on your mind helps you to deal with your emotions and worries. Often, when we feel self-doubt, we can feel worried about telling anybody.

Speaking about your challenges and feelings takes bravery, so when you share your worries, it makes sense to share them with someone you know and trust.

## How to spot a trusted grown-up

✦ You know them already

✦ You feel safe and calm around them

✦ They show respect and kindness in their actions

✦ They are good at listening

A trusted grown-up might be a parent, carer, teacher, aunt, uncle or any grown-up you know.

Who could be your trusted grown-up? Write their name here:

# I am BRAVE

## Activity: Mindful colouring

Colouring is a brilliant, mindful activity that can help us feel calm. Take a break to colour in this confidence-growing picture.

# Why going slowly grows confidence quicker

Sometimes, it seems like if we just ignored our feelings of fear and self-doubting thoughts, we could just leap into our challenges, get them done and our confidence levels would soar because we'd done something really brave.

And sometimes, like when there's an emergency, we have to do things before we feel ready.

But when we do something before we feel ready, it can feel so big and so scary, that our circle of confidence actually shrinks.

*Tom's big challenge is speaking on stage. He wants to read his lines at the end-of-year show with confidence, but when he gets up on the school stage, his confidence levels drop. His self-doubting thoughts tell him that he'll muddle his lines.*

*At the first performance, he decides to ignore his feelings and just go up on stage. But when he gets there, his feelings of fear and self-doubt are so big that his fears come true: he feels so anxious that he mixes up his lines.*

*Afterwards, Tom thinks his self-doubting thoughts were right. He decides never to go on stage again.*

## Part 2: How to grow your confidence

Can you see how Tom's circle of confidence got smaller? Now Tom doesn't feel confident even to try again.

When we go slowly and take our challenges one step at a time, we collect small, positive experiences that help our circle of confidence grow. Breaking down big challenges into smaller ones means each brave step builds on the last.

*Instead of ignoring his feelings, Tom takes the time to break his big challenge down. First, he talks to a trusted grown-up – his drama teacher. His drama teacher understands how Tom is feeling and helps him grow his confidence slowly.*

*Tom practises his lines with his teacher, rehearses being on stage without the audience and finds a mindful exercise to help him focus.*

*On the day of the next performance, Tom still needs bravery to go and read his lines, but his circle of confidence has stretched and grown. Tom's voice shakes a little at first, but then he remembers what he practised. He feels more confident and reads his lines with a loud, steady voice.*

# My feelings matter

# Confidence-boosting buddies

True friends will grow your confidence because they think you're awesome, even when you're struggling with self-doubt and low confidence.

We can have true friends, best friends, people we like and those we are friendly with. Not everybody can be true friends with each other, because it takes time to build a true friendship.

Just because someone spends time with you and says they are your friend, doesn't always make it true! Sometimes, someone might say they're your friend but not act like a friend at all. False friends are like bullies in disguise. They shrink your confidence and grow your feelings of self-doubt. Remember: you don't have to spend time with people who are unkind to you.

| A True Friend | A False Friend |
|---|---|
| Listens to you | Ignores you |
| Talks to you kindly | Teases or embarrasses you |
| Stands up for you | Hurts you |
| Includes you | Leaves you out |

# Activity: My friend would say...

Think of a true friend who thinks you're awesome. Imagine they are with you now. Draw them on the page and write down how they would describe you.

I love playing

with you

I always look forward
to seeing you because

You are really
good at

# Comparison is a confidence shrinker!

It's easy to see the best in our friends, but sometimes trickier to think kind thoughts about ourselves. When you're growing your confidence, it can be difficult to act with bravery and try your best when there are people around you who've already mastered the skill you're learning.

Remember, if someone can cycle faster, draw better or swim further than you, it's usually because they've had more practice. Take a break if you're feeling frustrated, but don't give up.

If you enjoy something, the fun you have when you are doing it is the important part. You don't need to be the best at everything!

And if there's an activity or hobby you love but are still learning to master, the best thing to do is more of it. Even experts were beginners first!

**Making mistakes means that you are trying, and we learn something new from each mistake we make.**

# My confidence tracker

When you're taking brave steps to grow your circle of confidence, it can help to keep a diary so you can keep track and see how your confidence is growing. Each time you do something that stretches your circle of confidence towards your challenge, use this tracker to keep a record of your progress.

Date:

My challenge:

My brave step:

How I felt:

What happened:

My confidence level:

# Part 2: How to grow your confidence

Date:

My challenge:

My brave step:

How I felt:

What happened:

My confidence level:

Date:

My challenge:

My brave step:

How I felt:

What happened:

My confidence level:

# Confident thoughts, self-doubting thoughts

True confidence comes from inside. Having confidence means feeling relaxed while being brave and knowing you'll be OK, even if things don't go perfectly.

Having low confidence means thoughts and feelings of fear and self-doubt stop you from feeling relaxed when you're doing something brave.

*Carina's dad wants her to go and play with her older cousins at a family party, but Carina's confidence levels drop when she's around older kids.*

*Her twin sister Niamh feels confident around older kids. Even though they don't see their cousins very often, she feels relaxed and OK about talking to them.*

Let's zoom in and see what's happening in Carina and Niamh's minds.

# Part 2: How to grow your confidence

Carina is having lots of self-doubting thoughts. These thoughts tell her that if she goes to talk to her older cousins, she will end up feeling embarrassed, rejected and alone.

Did you notice that Niamh's thoughts are confident, kind to herself and still have a little self-doubt? She feels a bit nervous, but brave enough to stretch her circle of confidence.

The good news is, you don't need to be 100 per cent super confident to do something brave. Thinking some confident thoughts will help shrink your self-doubt. Keep reading to find out more…

# Confident affirmations

If you struggle with low confidence, self-doubting thoughts can fill your mind up, squeezing out any confidence you might have had!

It might feel strange at first, but you can practise saying and thinking confident affirmations in order to shrink your self-doubting thoughts down to size. Adding some confident affirmations to your mind will help grow your confidence by giving your mind new, positive possibilities to think about.

Read or write these confident affirmations every day, taking a moment to say the words in your head, to help you think more positively about yourself:

I believe in myself

I am smart

I have the confidence to be myself

I can stand up for myself and my friends

I can speak my mind

I can take on challenges

My confidence is growing every day

I can achieve anything I put my mind to

I am full of potential

I always do my best

I am proud of myself

I can make a difference

I am resilient

I am a good friend to myself and others

I am unique and special

I challenge myself every day

I am important

I am strong

I can do this

I am brave

# Part 2: How to grow your confidence

Now, pick three of your favourites from that list and say them out loud with as much confidence as you can.

Lastly, pick one confident affirmation to write here. Make the letters as big as you can and take some time to colour and decorate your confident affirmation.

# What is assertiveness?

Assertiveness means being respectful to yourself as well as others. When someone is assertive they can think and make choices for themselves while also listening to others and showing respect.

It takes confidence to be assertive and it's not always easy! Acting with assertiveness means remembering that we deserve just as much respect as everybody else, and it can feel like a tricky balance sometimes.

*Aisha feels really hungry and pushes in front of Miriam in the queue at lunchtime. Miriam has lots of options for how she could respond to Aisha's actions.*

She probably deserves to eat her lunch before me

I'll ignore what just happened, I don't want to cause a fuss

That's not fair – I deserve to eat my lunch just as much as she does

Even if she's really hungry, it's not OK to push in without asking

Excuse me, I was here first

YOU PUSHED IN FRONT OF ME! YOU'RE A BAD PERSON!

Can you think of any other thoughts Miriam might have had? Add your ideas!

All of these responses make sense, but did you spot the assertive thought bubbles?

Even if she's really hungry, it's not OK to push in without asking

Excuse me, I was here first

Miriam considers why Aisha might have pushed in, recognizes that it's not kind towards herself to accept it and respectfully speaks up for herself. That's assertiveness and it's a brilliant way to practise acting with confidence.

# I can feel my confidence growing every day!

# Part 3:
# Shrinking self-doubt

Everybody has thoughts and feelings of self-doubt – it's part of being a human being. But when self-doubt stops us from finding our bravery and confidence, it's time to shrink it! In this chapter you'll learn how self-doubt works and how to shrink it so your confidence can grow.

# What are my self-doubting thoughts?

The first step in shrinking self-doubt is to spot your self-doubting thoughts. A self-doubting thought is a thought that tries to persuade us not to act with confidence. Self-doubting thoughts tell us not to take a chance, try new things or challenge ourselves.

Here are some of the most common self-doubting thoughts lots of people struggle with. Draw a circle around any that you recognize from your own mind.

People will laugh at me

They won't want to be my friend any more

I'll get it wrong

Someone will be angry with me

I'll ruin it

Nobody wants to hear from me

No one will understand

I'll be in danger

I'll get hurt

I'm not good enough

Everyone else is much better at this than me

People will be annoyed with me

If I ask for help, they'll think I'm stupid

I should already be good at this

**If none of these feel familiar, you can write your own below:**

_____

_____

Of course, sometimes our brains tell us not to take a risk because we truly would be endangering ourselves, unnecessarily upsetting others or perhaps we're simply not ready yet. Taking some deep breaths to calm our minds and bodies can help us tell if our thoughts are based in sensible reality or self-doubt.

# Activity: True or false?

Now we're going to be detectives. Pick one of the self-doubting thoughts you chose. We're going to investigate…

To help with this activity, you can ask yourself these questions:

*Am I being fair to myself?* E.g. Is it fair to think my friends will stop liking me?

*Is it helpful to me to think this?* E.g. Is it helpful to picture myself ruining everything?

*Is it likely that it's true?* E.g. Is it likely that someone will be angry at me for trying my best?

*Is it based on facts?* E.g. Am I 100 per cent certain people will laugh at me?

*What facts prove this thought wrong?*

*Would I say this thought to my best friend?*

Investigate your thought and put your findings here!

| Thought | Findings | Is the thought true? |
|---|---|---|
| I should already be good at this | It takes loads of practice to get good at something | No! |
|  |  |  |

# I'm awesome exactly as I am

# Thought mix-ups

Self-doubting thoughts are often thought mix-ups. A thought mix-up is when your brain is trying really hard to stop you from doing something that feels scary or challenging, so it invents stories to persuade you not to act with bravery.

The truth is, our brains really like to feel safe and calm, so acting with bravery can be very difficult. That's where thought mix-ups come in – here are all the different types:

### All-or-nothing thinking:
If something isn't perfect, I've failed completely

### Over-generalizing:
If one thing goes wrong, everything will go wrong

### Focusing on the negatives:
I can only think about the things that go wrong

### Fortune-telling:
I know everything will go wrong

### Mind-reading:
I know everyone thinks badly of me

### Catastrophic thinking:
If I make one mistake I will ruin everything

65

**Magnified thinking:**
The things I dislike about myself are the most important things about me. The things I like about myself aren't important

**Negative comparison:**
My friend is better than me in every way

**Unrealistic expectations:**
I should be perfect all the time, I shouldn't need help

**Putting yourself down:**
I'm so annoying

**Blaming yourself:**
Everything goes wrong and it's all my fault

**Feelings are facts:**
I feel embarrassed, everyone must be laughing at me

**Do any of these sound like the voice you talk to yourself with? Draw a circle round any you recognize.**

# I can make a difference

# Thinking confident!

While we can't choose the emotions we feel, we can choose to add confident thoughts to our minds. It takes time to begin believing new thoughts, but in time, confident thoughts feel more comfortable and we start to think them without having to try. As our thoughts slowly change, our feelings and circle of confidence can change too.

Think of your mind like a paint pot. If your mind is full of blue, self-doubting thoughts, a confident thought is like a drop of yellow paint. Mixing in one drop makes a tiny difference, and the more you add yellow drops, the more your mind turns green.

Use coloured pens or pencils to colour in one circle blue and one circle yellow. Where they overlap, the colours mix to make green!

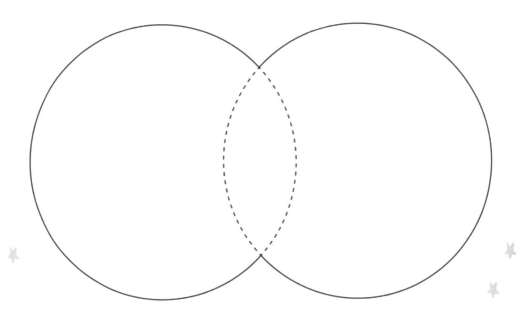

# Transform your thoughts!

The best way to choose confident thoughts is to think about how you can be kind to yourself and your emotions.

| Self-doubting thought | How I feel | Confident thought |
|---|---|---|
| People will laugh at me | Scared of embarrassment | If I'm not perfect, I'll be OK |
| I'll get it wrong | Scared of failure | I can go at my own pace |
| Someone will be annoyed with me | Scared of upsetting others | It's OK to try my best, I don't need to be perfect |
| I'll ruin it for everyone | Scared of disappointing others | I can practise and each time I do, it will get easier |
| Everyone else is better than me | Worthless | Everyone is different, it's OK to be me |
| I should already be good at this | Annoyed at myself | Everybody has to begin somewhere, I'm OK |

# Activity:
# Creating confident thoughts

Now it's your turn! Each time a self-doubting thought pops into your head and tries to stop you from doing something, write it down here. Can you work out how you're feeling? How can you turn it into a confident thought?

If you get stuck, think about the super confident superhero self you designed on page 28. What would they say to you?

| Self-doubting thought | How I feel | Confident thought |
|---|---|---|
|  |  |  |
|  |  |  |
|  |  |  |

# It's OK to feel what I'm feeling

# Being kind to yourself

A big part of being confident is feeling sure you'll be OK, even if things don't go perfectly. One way we can always make sure we'll be OK is by being kind to ourselves.

When you take the time to think kind thoughts and show yourself kind actions, self-doubting thoughts lose their power.

How can you show yourself kindness today?

Cuddle a soft blanket

Have a drink of water

Talk about your feelings

Give yourself a hug

Practise mindfulness exercises and affirmations

Say some kind words to yourself

# How to be your own best friend

Being a best friend to yourself takes practice, but it's quite simple. There are lots of different ways to show yourself friendship, but if you do these three things, you'll be your own best friend:

**1.** **Be kind to yourself when you make a mistake**

**2.** **Make time to do the things you enjoy**

**3.** **Speak up for yourself when you need help or something is unfair**

If you can remember to do these three things for yourself, you will always have a safe and friendly place to go – your own mind! When you know for sure that you always have yourself for a friend, it becomes easier to find bravery and grow your confidence.

Just like learning any skill, thinking kind, confident thoughts can be tricky at first. Don't worry when you have a self-doubting thought, it doesn't mean you've failed. Everyone has them, even people who seem happy and confident all the time. Each time a negative thought pops up, remind yourself that it is just a thought and not a truth and see it as an opportunity to practise thinking confidently. Before you know it, you'll be an expert.

# Dealing with criticism

Remember the growth mindset idea we learned about on page 31? When we have a growth mindset, we know we are always learning and changing. One of the ways we learn and change is when others show us how we might be able to get even better – this is called constructive criticism or feedback.

*Frida has written a story about two cats who go on an adventure. She's really proud of it and shows it to her teacher. Her teacher loves the story! She wants to help Frida make the story the best it can be, and the teacher shows Frida which chapters she thinks Frida could work on to make the story even more brilliant.*

*Even though it hurts a bit to hear criticism, Frida understands that her teacher speaks with respect and is showing that she believes in Frida's story.*

# Part 3: Shrinking self-doubt

Kind and respectful criticism helps us grow! Here's how to handle it when it feels difficult:

Sometimes, people aren't as respectful as Frida's teacher, and they can give criticism without using kindness or respect. This hurts even more and can shrink our confidence!

Everybody has different opinions and a unique view. If someone is unkind or disrespectful about something you're trying your best with, it's OK to ignore them – you don't have to take on criticism that isn't given with respect. Be kind to yourself and keep growing your confidence!

# I Like Myself journal

Take some time every day to write some kind, confident words to yourself. These journal pages will help get you started. If you want to carry on, all you need is a notebook and a pen or pencil!

Write in your "I Like Myself" journal every day for a week…

Today I…

I was proud of myself when…

A difficult part of today was when…

Today I showed myself kindness when…

Today I…

I was proud of myself when…

A difficult part of today was when…

Today I showed myself kindness when…

# Part 3: Shrinking self-doubt

Today I...

_____

I was proud of myself when...

_____

A difficult part of today was when...

_____

Today I showed myself kindness when...

_____

---

Today I...

_____

I was proud of myself when...

_____

A difficult part of today was when...

_____

Today I showed myself kindness when...

_____

---

Today I...

_____

I was proud of myself when...

_____

A difficult part of today was when...

_____

Today I showed myself kindness when...

_____

Today I...

I was proud of myself when...

A difficult part of today was when...

Today I showed myself kindness when...

Today I...

I was proud of myself when...

A difficult part of today was when...

Today I showed myself kindness when...

When you make time to look for ways to be kind to yourself every day, your brain gets more used to it – and more skilled at finding kindness!

# Activity: My confidence jar

Did you know that we're more likely to remember unkind words than kind ones? Taking a moment to write down and collect kind words, proud moments and achievements – big or small – will make sure you have a store of confidence-boosting, self-doubt-shrinking moments to turn to whenever you need them.

To make a confidence jar, all you need is a jar or small box, a pen or pencil and scissors.

Begin by writing some kind words, proud moments and achievements in the squares – can you think of nine to start you off?

# GROW YOUR CONFIDENCE

Keep adding to your confidence jar! Whenever you have a confidence-boosting moment, write it down on a piece of paper and pop it in.

Now cut out your confidence-boosting moments (ask a grown-up for help using scissors), fold them in half and keep them in your jar or box. Each time something good happens that you want to make sure you remember, write it down and put it in the jar with your other confident moments.

Any time you're having trouble with self-doubt, read a piece of paper from the jar and it will give you a little boost of confidence.

# I am always learning

# Activity: Confidence word search

You're learning so much and doing so incredibly well! Let's take a break with some fun puzzles.

```
G B L E W O V B X P A L E W Q P
F L P W O M B I R F G K Q O X O
U L D K E P L G M V K Q O D D W
N K R C O N F I D E N T A O V E
I F R B H U J M I O L B P X R R
Q P M H Y F E I L W C X R P N F
U T O A P C R S T W U N O W O U
E B J P K O L T C X E A U F B L
C I K P V T R U D R E M D P L S
L P O Y Y T V R W S X Z A Q N U
K O H T N R E D C V X W H M K O
V D N I K D R E F W P Q E T D C
M U I T R E X Q G R O W J Y T P
```

CONFIDENT    PROUD    GROW    POWERFUL
HAPPY        KIND     UNIQUE

# Part 3: Shrinking self-doubt

Can you help the superhero find their cape?

Solving puzzles is a fantastic way to enjoy spending time with yourself, and cracking the puzzles gives you a brilliant boost of confidence too!

# My best
# is best
# for me

# Part 4: Quick confidence hacks

You've learned a lot about how to grow your confidence slowly and steadily, and shrink down your self-doubt at the same time. But what about those times when you need a boost of confidence in a hurry? Whether you need to stand up for a friend or try something new, in this chapter you'll find all sorts of ideas for finding confidence when you need it most.

# What is empathy?

Empathy is the skill of imagining how others are feeling. For example, at your friend's birthday party you can imagine they feel excited and perhaps a little nervous about being the centre of attention – that's empathy!

Empathy can help us find confidence quickly because when we take the time to imagine how others are feeling, it reminds us that nobody is perfect and most people are kind.

*Robin has joined a football club, and it's his first time meeting his teammates. He feels very nervous and is having self-doubting thoughts about whether they'll like him.*

*Robin uses empathy to imagine how his teammates might be feeling.*

# Part 4: Quick confidence hacks

Often, when we feel a lot of self-doubt and our confidence is low, we think that others are super confident and will be unkind to us. When we take a moment to use empathy, we realize that other people have their own worries and that they might even be feeling the same self-doubt we are.

Next time you're feeling low on confidence, take a moment to use your empathy and imagination.

## How am I feeling?

_____

_____

## Who are the other people I am worrying about?

_____

_____

## When I use my empathy and imagination, I think they might be feeling and thinking…

_____

_____

_____

# Imagine your success

Lots of professional athletes and sportspeople use a technique called visualization to give them confidence when they have a big game or competition to prepare for. They use their imaginations to see themselves winning, which helps their brains get comfortable with the idea and actually increases their chances of doing well on the day!

Olympic medal-winning swimmer Katie Ledecky says she uses visualization to win swimming races. She doesn't just think about how the race will look, she imagines how her body will feel at each point.

Whatever you need to boost your confidence for, you can use visualization to help you feel ready and positive. Here's how to do it:

1. Close your eyes and take some deep breaths.

2. Picture yourself in the situation, imagining all the details you can.

3. Like a video game or movie, imagine going through the situation step by step, and imagine it going really well.

4. See if you can feel the emotions you'll feel when you succeed.

# Stand tall

How we hold our bodies has a big effect on how confident we feel. Simply changing how you are standing or sitting can give you a quick boost of confidence.

Try it now!

Can you feel a boost of confidence when you hold your body in this way?

# GROW YOUR CONFIDENCE

Try these confidence-boosting poses next! You can practise them in the morning to start your day off with confidence, or just before facing a challenge.

# Breathe yourself confident

You breathe all day and night, mostly without thinking about it. When we feel nervous, low in confidence and full of self-doubt, our breaths become short and shallow, and we don't take as much oxygen into our bodies.

Taking deep breaths helps calm our bodies and brains, making us feel more confident, resilient and capable.

A long, slow, deep breath will always help you feel a little calmer and more in control. On the next few pages, you'll find some breathing exercises specially designed to boost your confidence – give them a try and see which ones feel good to you.

## Breathing track

Place your finger at the start line, and slowly trace it around the race track. As your finger moves around the first loop, breathe in. Breathe out as your finger traces the second loop.

Start

When you want to breathe for a boost of confidence, you can use this book, draw a track yourself or trace the shape on the palm of your hand!

# Double nose breathing

Sometimes, when it's time to act with bravery and find confidence, we can feel very anxious. This breathing exercise is especially good for calming feelings of anxiety.

1. Close your eyes and take a breath in through your nose.

2. Instead of breathing out, take another breath in.

3. Now slowly breathe out through your mouth.

4. Repeat three times.

Notice how you feel after three double-nose breaths. Tick which you're experiencing:

- [ ] Calmer

- [ ] Slower heartbeat

- [ ] More confident

- [ ] Less busy thoughts

- [ ] Less anxious feelings

- [ ] More positive thoughts

# Hot chocolate breathing

Here's a yummy breathing exercise to get you feeling ready for anything:

1. Imagine you are holding a mug of hot chocolate in front of you, with all your favourite toppings.

2. Take a deep breath in through your nose, smelling the delicious aroma of the hot chocolate.

3. Now breathe out through your mouth, imagining you are blowing on the drink to cool it down.

Colour in this mug of hot chocolate and add toppings!

# I can take a deep breath!

# Shake it off

Have you ever noticed how dogs and cats have a good shake after something stressful or frightening happens? It's their way of letting the tension and stress out of their bodies, and it works for humans too!

Next time you feel nervous or tense about something and you want a boost of confidence and positivity, try shaking, wriggling and jiggling your body for 5 seconds.

# Make a glitter jar to shake with you!

Shake up your glitter jar and watch the glitter go bananas inside! As you watch the glitter move more slowly and calmly, you'll feel yourself relax too.

## You will need:

- Clean, empty jar with a tight lid
- Water
- 2 tbsp biodegradable glitter

## How to:

1. Pour the glitter carefully into the jar, followed by the water.
2. Replace the lid firmly – ask a grown-up to help make sure it's on really tight so there are no spills!
3. Shake your body and your glitter jar next time you want to release some tension to feel calm and confident.

# Choose a confident story

Self-doubting thoughts come up with all kinds of negative stories. They make us believe that we're not good enough, and that it's not worth acting with bravery because things might go wrong and we risk feeling embarrassed or hurt.

We can choose to tell ourselves confident stories – positive ones that can give us hope and resilience.

Next time your mind gets busy with self-doubting thoughts, take some time to think about a confident story instead.

Below are some self-doubting stories and some confident stories – can you draw a circle around the confident stories?

If I mess up, everybody will laugh at me

If I make a mistake, I'll be OK – trying my best is enough

I'm sure I'll lose the game, I'm not going to go

I could win, and either way I'll have fun

I can feel nervous
and act with bravery,
I've got this

I feel too
nervous
to do this

Standing up for
myself is brave
and important

If I stand up for
myself they'll be angry
with me, I'll stay quiet

They probably won't
want to be my
friend

I wonder if
we're a good fit
for friendship

# Be yourself

We all have a picture in our minds of someone who is super confident, but the truth is, everybody can be confident. You can be confident and quiet, confident and funny, confident and *you*.

If you're reading this book and you think you need to change yourself into a confident person, think again. It's very difficult to act with confidence if you are also trying to act like you are somebody else.

Self-doubting thoughts often tell us that it's not OK to be ourselves. They tell us if we simply go to the party and be ourselves, or start talking to a new friend about what's fascinating to us, or stand up for ourselves and speak with honesty, then something bad will happen.

Real, true confidence means being ourselves and being brave at the same time. If something is difficult for you and you don't feel confident about it, that's OK. As we learned in Part 2, growing confidence takes time and practice – no one is 100 per cent confident at everything (not even grown-ups).

Wherever your confidence levels are, it's OK to be you.

# Part 4: Quick confidence hacks

Take some time to celebrate yourself with a self-portrait! Draw yourself here doing something you love:

# I am confident, I am me!

Yoga stretches help us release tension, breathe more deeply and feel more confident. Next time you have a big day ahead of you, start your morning with these yoga poses:

## Mountain

Begin by standing tall like a mountain.
This position makes you feel calm and strong.

## Warrior

Take a big, confident step forward and bend your front knee. Put your palms together and reach up high. This pose makes you feel ready for anything.

# Tree

Stretch your arms up to the sky and balance on one leg with the other leg bent and your foot connecting to the supporting leg. This one is challenging – doing our best when faced with a challenge grows confidence!

# Star

Spread your arms and feet wide so you are shaped like a star! This stretch makes you feel big, steady and powerful.

# Challenges help me grow

# Part 5:
# Taking care of you

Growing your confidence is hard work, and you should be very proud of yourself. Taking good care of our minds and bodies is a big part of feeling relaxed and confident when facing challenges.

Treating our bodies with care and respect is something we can do every day. In this chapter you'll find lots of ideas for looking after yourself.

# A good night's sleep

Sleeping well gives us confidence because when we sleep our minds and bodies can recharge. Without this time to rest and relax, it's much harder to think clearly and positively, and our bodies feel tired.

Think of yourself like a battery that needs charging up overnight. If you don't get properly charged, you have less energy the next day. When you have a good amount of charge in your energy battery, you're better able to find the bravery to face challenges and grow your confidence.

# My bedroom

As sleep is so important, it makes sense that where you sleep is important too! Everybody is different, so the things that make you feel relaxed and ready to sleep will be unique to you.

Can you draw your bedroom below, including all the things that help you feel comfy and cosy at bedtime?

# My bedtime routine

To wind down and have a great, confidence-growing night's sleep, it helps to have a bedtime routine. Doing the same things in the same order each night helps our minds and bodies understand that it's time to relax and rest.

## Ramin's bedtime routine

**Have a shower**

**Brush my teeth**

**Read a chapter of my book**

**Hug my mum and dad goodnight**

**Turn out the light**

**Go to sleep**

What's your bedtime routine?

_____    _____

_____    _____

_____    _____

_____    _____

# Talking about feelings

One of the best ways to take care of our minds and emotions is to talk about our feelings with our friends and trusted grown-ups. When we share how we're feeling, our emotions get lighter and our loved ones get to know us better.

If you don't feel confident talking about your feelings, these handy phrases might help get you started.

Can I talk to you about something I feel shy about?

Do you ever worry about...?

I'm reading this book called Grow Your Confidence, can I show you?

I feel silly saying this, but...

You always seem so confident, have you always been that way?

Something's bothering me, can I tell you about it?

I need your help solving a problem

# Move your body

Our bodies are amazing and they love to move! Dancing, climbing, running, walking, jumping… all sorts of movement and exercise help keep our bodies healthy and make our brains produce feel-good chemicals. These chemicals make you feel happier and more confident – giving you a brilliant boost!

Can you draw yourself joining in with these active kids?

# Being in nature

Getting outdoors and into nature helps calm your mind and body. When we breathe fresh air, slow down and notice the beauty all around us, we can relax, recharge and feed our imagination.

Next time you go out into nature – whether it's a local park, beach, lake or forest – try and spot everything on this fun scavenger hunt list. When you spot each one, take a moment to look at it carefully and notice all its small details – there's a space to draw each item on the opposite page.

☐ Something that has fallen from a tree

☐ Something with a soft texture

☐ A footprint

☐ An insect

☐ A Y-shaped stick

☐ An interesting stone

☐ Something with spots

☐ A flower

☐ Something yellow

# Part 5: Taking care of you

Draw the items here as you spot them:

# I can ask for help

# Go bananas

Your body needs a mix of foods to help you grow strong and keep your mind and body feeling good.

Bananas are one of the best foods for boosting confidence because they help your brain produce feel-good chemicals called dopamine and serotonin. They also give you energy and taste great!

Of course, you can eat a banana as it is, but if you want to try something special, here's a recipe for delicious, creamy banana ice cream:

## You will need:

- ☆ One ripe banana per person
- ☆ 1 tbsp milk per person
  (cow, goat or plant-based)
- ☆ Blender
- ☆ Optional extras: cocoa powder,
  nut butter, cinnamon,
  frozen berries

# How to:

1. Ask an adult to help you peel and carefully slice the bananas.

2. Place the slices on a tray or in a bag and freeze for at least 3 hours.

3. Once frozen, put your banana slices in the blender with the milk (ask a grown-up for help using the blender) – add cocoa powder or nut butter if you're using it.

4. Blend until smooth and creamy.

5. Stir through cinnamon or berries, if using.

6. Serve and enjoy!

# It's OK to be different

Suppose the other children in your class all think cake is the best food, but you love ice cream. Who is right? Neither... and both! You don't have to think the same as everyone else. Friends don't have to agree on everything – in fact, it's much more interesting when people have different opinions.

No two human beings are exactly alike, even twins! We are all unique and special, and you'll have some things in common and some differences with each person you meet.

Don't be afraid to disagree... or to change your mind. You can speak your mind and say how you really feel, even if sometimes it takes bravery to do so. Expressing your true thoughts and feelings is an important part of showing yourself care and respect.

Can you think of something you've disagreed with a friend about?

Can you think of something you've changed your mind about?

# It's great to be me

# Stay hydrated!

Did you know that our bodies are made up of on average 60 per cent water? Almost every part of our bodies needs water in order to work properly, so when we're thirsty, it affects everything – including our confidence!

If you want a quick, easy boost of confidence, have a glass of water. Even better, make sure you drink plenty of water throughout the day to keep your brain and body working well. You can add extra ingredients to water to make it even more amazing – try these delicious ideas:

# Finding balance

Growing your confidence and facing challenges is hard work! It's important to balance challenging yourself with doing things that are fun and relaxing for you. Mohammed has created a good balance between relaxing and facing challenges:

Can you find a good balance between your relaxing activities and your challenges?

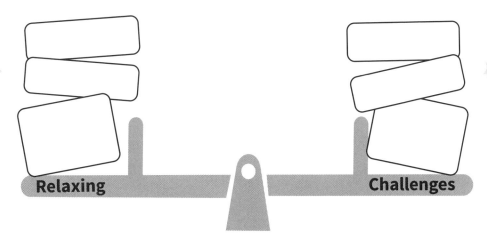

# Play is powerful

We grow our confidence really well when we play. Making our challenges into a fun game rather than taking them very seriously means that we're more able to relax and find bravery.

You can make just about anything into a fun, playful activity – the most important part is to take away any pressure. When we play, we need to be able to experiment and try new things without having to worry about it – that's what makes play fun.

Here are some ideas for making your challenges into playful fun:

- ☆ Practise role-playing with your friends or a trusted grown-up – e.g. you could pretend to be your teacher and your grown-up could be you asking them for help – then swap!

- ☆ Do something similar that you find fun and easy – e.g. if visiting another country is a challenge, try taking a trip to a nearby town

- ☆ Watch a film, play a game or read a book where a character faces a similar challenge. Daydream about being just like the character

# Part 5: Taking care of you

Here's an example of using play to grow your confidence. If you're practising the skill of thinking positively and having a growth mindset, this puzzle is for you.

Unscrambling the letters in the positive words and statements, instead of just reading them, gives your brain a fun challenge, which helps it learn faster and remember the positive ideas more clearly.

If you get stuck, turn to page 141 for the answers!

**NRLAE** _____

**ROWG** _____

**TYR NAIGA** _____

**DO YM STBE** _____

**IRCPTECA** _____

**LSCGLNEAEH** _____

**VBEEELI** _____

**I ANC DO TI** _____

**VRAERYB** _____

**FDEOCINTN** _____

# Your amazing body

Your body is amazing! It is made up of 17 trillion cells that all work together to keep you breathing, laughing, singing and dancing. Your heart beats over 100,000 times every day. Messages travel through your nerves to your brain at speeds of up to 170 miles per hour.

Your body changes as you get older and start to grow into an adult, which might make you feel worried, confused or embarrassed. Everyone goes through these changes, so whatever you're experiencing, you're definitely not the only one.

We find confidence in our bodies when we treat them with respect. Your body is precious and it belongs to you. You can always talk to your trusted grown-up about anything that's troubling you.

# Planet Perfect

A lot of the people we see on TV and online look like aliens from Planet Perfect, and this can be a confidence shrinker if we worry that we should look perfect too. Did you know that special lights and editing tricks are used to make them look perfect on screen? In real life, famous people are just human beings with unique and imperfect faces and bodies.

If someone tries to make you feel bad because of how you look, it's not your body, face, clothes or hair that needs to change, it's their level of respect.

Remember that if someone is being disrespectful to you, it's probably because they don't feel good or confident about themselves.

# I am
# brave

# Part 6:
# Looking to the future

We've nearly reached the end of this book! Hopefully the activities have helped you grow your confidence and given you some of the skills to build it. Well done! You have achieved a lot.

Now that you know all about confidence and how to grow it, you can use what you've learned every day. Turn the page to find out how...

# Grow your confidence cheat sheet

You've learned so much about confidence, bravery, thoughts and feelings! Here's a cheat sheet with some of the most important ideas and tools from this book. When you want to grow your confidence quickly, turn to this page!

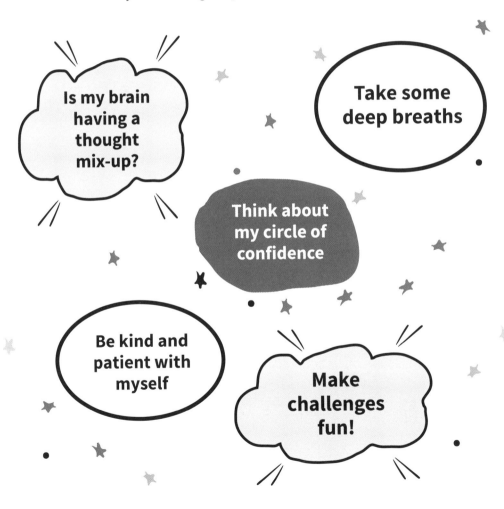

**Is my brain having a thought mix-up?**

**Take some deep breaths**

**Think about my circle of confidence**

**Be kind and patient with myself**

**Make challenges fun!**

# My top tips for growing confidence

Now you've learned all about growing confidence, what are your top tips? They might be from this book, something you've come up with yourself or something you've been told about.

Write your top tips here:

_____

_____

_____

_____

_____

_____

_____

_____

# I can shrink my self-doubt

## Farewell

You've reached the end of *Grow Your Confidence* – well done! You've learned some amazing things, and it makes sense if it all feels like quite a lot of information. You can go back and read this book again or skip to the part you're interested in at any time.

You are brave, brilliant and capable of overcoming challenges. You are becoming a wonderful friend to yourself, which will help you through life's ups and downs. Every day you are growing your confidence, and by doing your best you are making a positive difference in the world.

# I can grow my confidence!

# For parents and carers: How to help your child grow their confidence

Supporting your child's confidence is all about balance. The balance between showing them they are loved and valued exactly as they are and challenging them to grow. Balancing their independence with your support and encouragement. You know your child better than anyone, and you can trust yourself to navigate that balance throughout their childhood.

One of the most powerful things you can do as a parent or carer is to set a good example. Show your child that you can feel unsure and do it anyway – that's true bravery and the key to confidence at any age.

Talk about your feelings and challenges in a way that lets your child know that we all struggle sometimes, and that there are things we can do to help calm ourselves and find our confidence. Vocalize your thought processes using positive, compassionate and solution-based language. And when you can, let them know just how good it feels when you conquer a fear.

It can be tempting to try and inflate your child's confidence with lots of praise. As parents and carers, we know just how special and brilliant our children are, and it hurts when they can't see it in themselves. However, too much praise can have the opposite of its intended effect – especially if it's mostly focused on results. True confidence comes not from a focus on getting praised by others, but from trusting ourselves, experimentation and trying our best.

Instead, try to be specific with your praise and focus on the process. Pick out what they did that you want to show genuine admiration for. Here are some examples:

- Things you know are challenging for them
- Using their imagination and creativity

- Learning from mistakes
- Perseverance and resilience
- Small improvements

Show them that their feelings really matter to you and that you understand their strengths and challenges. Even when they seem to take a step back, show that you are proud of them for not giving up and explore how they could learn from the setback – these are often the most valuable learning experiences of all.

Peer pressure can ramp up around this age, and it takes huge strength of character to be yourself in the face of it. While you have to let your child find their own way among their peers, at home show them how much you value their uniqueness as well as their developing personality. Always let them know that it's OK to feel different (ironically, it's one of the things most young people have in common with one another), and it's OK to find things hard. Try to encourage them gently towards positive and diverse role models, and feed their imagination with inspiring books, films and experiences.

Sometimes, your child might come to you with a problem they'd like your help solving, but more often what they need from you is a listening ear and a shoulder to cry on. Showing them that you are always on their team will give them the confidence to strike out and try new things. They'll feel safe in the knowledge that you'll be there for them, whether they succeed with flying colours or find it more difficult than they imagined, and especially when they fail.

I hope this book has been useful for you and your child. It's always hard to see your child struggling, shrinking back or missing out due to a lack of confidence, and you're doing a great job by taking an active interest in their emotional well-being. In doing so you are showing them how to treat themselves with care and respect, which will give them the resilience to take chances and grow into courageous young people.

# Further advice

Low confidence doesn't feel nice, but it is normal. If you have serious concerns about how your child's thoughts and feelings are affecting their life and mental health, it's best to start by talking to your doctor and your child's school. The following organizations also offer advice, information and support:

### YoungMinds' free parent helpline:
0808 802 5544

### Mind:
www.mind.org.uk
0300 123 3393
info@mind.org.uk

### Childline:
www.childline.org.uk
0800 1111

### NHS Choices:
www.nhs.uk/mental-health

### BBC Bitesize Parents' toolkit:
www.bbc.co.uk/bitesize/parents

### Child Mind Institute (USA):
www.childmind.org

### Mental Health America:
www.mhanational.org

# Recommended reading

**For kids:**
*Happy, Healthy Minds*
The School of Life

*Stand Up for Yourself & Your Friends*
Patti Kelley Criswell

*Wreck This Journal*
Keri Smith

**For adults:**
*It's OK Not to Share*
Heather Shumaker

*The Book You Wish Your Parents Had Read*
Philippa Perry

*The Story Cure*
Ella Berthoud and Susan Elderkin

# Answers for the activities

## p. 82

```
G B L E W O V B X P A L E W Q P
F L P W O M B I R F G K Q O X O
U L D K E P L G M V K Q O D D W
N K R C O N F I D E N T A O V E
I F R B H U J M I O L B P X R R
Q P M H Y F E I L W C X R P N F
U T O A P C R S T W U N O W O U
E B J P K O L T C X E A U F B L
C I K P V T R U D R E M D P L S
L P O Y Y T V R W S X Z A Q N U
K O H T N R E D C V X W H M K O
V D N I K D R E F W P Q E T D C
M U I T R E X Q G R O W J Y T P
```

## p. 83

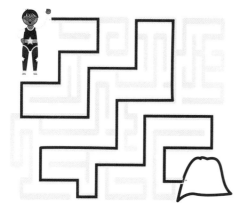

## p. 125

LEARN, GROW, TRY AGAIN, DO MY BEST, PRACTICE, CHALLENGES, BELIEVE, I CAN DO IT, BRAVERY, CONFIDENT

# Shrink Your Worries

**978-1-83799-172-3**

### A worry-busting guide to help 7+-year-olds
### calm anxious thoughts and fears

Worry is a part of being human, but high levels of stress and anxiety can hold your child back. Equipping children with coping strategies to tackle worries enables them to be their calmest, most content selves.

Encourage your child to listen to their feelings, practise positive thinking and overcome their fears with this sensitive and supportive book. Bursting with fun activities, handy tips and simple exercises, *Shrink Your Worries* is the self-care companion every stress-prone child needs.

# My Emotions and Me

978-1-80007-994-6

**A stunning and playful graphic novel exploring emotions and how to cope with them, for everyone from 7 to 107!**

Did you know:
- When you're experiencing a feeling, it's much easier to feel the emotion rather than put it into words?
- The four basic emotions – anger, joy, sadness and fear – all have a positive function?
- You can ease intense feelings by inviting them into your body, and with some deep breathing you can feel calm again?

Join Art-mella and her furry sidekick Rattie as they go on a fascinating voyage of self-discovery where they learn all about emotions; why we have them, how we process them and techniques on how to cope with them.

Have you enjoyed this book?
If so, why not write a review on your favourite website?

If you're interested in finding out more about our books,
find us on Facebook at **Summersdale Publishers**,
on Twitter/X at **@Summersdale** and on Instagram and
TikTok at **@summersdalebooks** and get in touch.
We'd love to hear from you!

Thanks very much for buying this Summersdale book.

# www.summersdale.com

## Image Credits

Illustrations of people by Wendy Middleditch; p.12 and elsewhere – background © Marf/Shutterstock.
com; p.16 – fingerprint © Alexandr III/Shutterstock.com; pp.18, 34, 53 – energy bars © EvGenius98/
Shutterstock.com; pp.31–32 © Whale Design/Shutterstock.com; p.43 © Panda Vector/Shutterstock.com;
p.45 © mirajeee/Shutterstock.com; pp.83 and 141 – maze © Haosame/Shutterstock.com; p.90
© MaryCo/Shutterstock.com; p.92 – track © Olenapolll/Shutterstock.com; p.94 © lichtfarbe/
Shutterstock.com; p.123 – see-saw © Blaka suta/Shutterstock.com; p.134 © mirajeee/Shutterstock.com